Making Ice Cream
and Frozen Yogurt

Maggie Oster

CONTENTS

Making Ice Cream and Frozen Yogurt

For me, ice cream is synonymous with late-night snacks, a tradition in my family. For others, apple pie may not be complete without a scoop of vanilla on top. For still others, ice cream may be identified with birthdays, summer Sunday afternoons, family reunions, the local dairy bar, 29 flavors, triple scoops, banana splits, hot fudge sundaes, or any number of other assorted associations. In any case, when you think of ice cream, likely you think of good times.

Ice cream and its various relatives, including ice milk, sherbet, sorbet, ice, and frozen yogurt, are America's favorite dessert — likewise, more of these treats are consumed in this country than anywhere else in the world. Today, ice cream knows no social boundaries, but early in its recorded history it was a food of royalty.

Nero had snow brought from the mountains to make ices flavored with fruits. In the 13th century, Marco Polo brought recipes for ices from China. The Italians took it to culinary heights, and from there it spread to the courts of France and England.

Ice cream arrived in North America in the 1700s. George and Martha Washington had ice cream made for them at Mount Vernon after being introduced to the confection by Mrs. Alexander Hamilton. Thomas Jefferson brought back recipes from his sojourns in France, but it was Dolly Madison who first served it in the White House.

What made ice cream readily accessible, however, was the invention of the ice cream churn, complete with dasher, hand crank, two tubs, ice, and salt, by a woman named Nancy Johnson in 1846. By 1851 ice cream was produced commercially. Ice cream sodas became an American mainstay after the Centennial Exposition in Philadelphia in 1879. That ubiquitous treat, the ice cream cone, came on the scene in 1904 at the St. Louis Exposition.

With the 20th century came widespread use of refrigeration, electricity, supermarkets, and convenience foods. Sure, it was fun to make ice cream at home on a summer day, but it was much easier to buy a neatly packaged half-gallon. Homemade ice cream became a delicacy for special occasions. We came to accept commercially made ice creams and other frozen desserts as good. Over a period of time what was once a simple mixture of milk, sweetener, flavoring, and possibly eggs, became a frozen chemical soup of over 60 additives with almost 50 percent more air than in homemade ice cream.

As we become more and more aware today of the real and potential harm of many of these "food" chemicals, we reach the point of either doing without or making our own.

For me, making ice cream at home always had a great deal of mystique. Recipe books warned that the proportion of salt and ice had to be just right for the mixture to freeze correctly. Use too much sugar and the mixture wouldn't freeze, too little and it would freeze hard as a brickbat. Writers warned of ice crystals and who knows what other plagues and evils. Many encouraged the use of perfectly good ingredients like gelatin and flour, but somehow these seemed alien to such a simple delight. Because I live alone, the usual freezer size of a half-gallon was much more of one flavor than I wanted. Finally, there was the thought of the mess of all that salt and dripping ice.

But one day I summoned up my culinary courage and made a mixture of fresh strawberries and honey, mashed them together, cooked it briefly, and stirred in some half-and-half. Then I put it in the deep freezer. Just like that, no magic incantations, no anything. Later that day I sampled the concoction. The result was sensational. Yes, there were ice crystals and the texture was less than creamy, but the flavor! Like nothing that ever came off a food technologist's shelf. A whole new world opened up for me.

Simply put, making ice cream and other frozen desserts yourself makes good sense and is a lot of fun. The flavors you can make are literally limitless, and the ingredients are readily available. Your ice cream will cost less than the premium brands and be vastly superior to the cheaper brands. Most importantly, you can control what goes into your ice cream, making it as sinfully rich or as austerely sliming as you want, with no unnecessary ingredients. If you decide to use an ice cream freezer, new ones are available in a wide range of sizes, are relatively inexpensive, and are easier than ever to use.

Homemade ice cream need no longer be a "once-in-the-summer" treat. Why not enjoy it year round?

The Ingredients

The basic ingredients of ice cream include a dairy product such as cream or milk, a sweetener, and a flavoring. By making your own ice cream you can interchange ingredients to suit your tastes and resources.

Milk Products

These provide protein as well as certain vitamins and minerals. Depending on which dairy product is used, this can be where the "bad buys," butterfat and calories, show up. The richer the ingredients, the richer and smoother the final product, but homemade, low-calorie frozen desserts are not in any way second-rate. Furthermore, they can be truly low-calorie, unlike many commercially made ice milks and frozen yogurts that have nearly as many calories as ice cream.

Having your own cow or goat means an abundant supply of fresh milk and is ideal in terms of wholesomeness, availability, and cost. But purchased milk products will also yield a better product than store-bought ice cream, and you'll still save money. For strict vegetarians, ice cream, sherbet, and frozen yogurt can be made from soy milk.

Whipping cream. With 36 percent butterfat, this naturally makes the creamiest dessert with that superb cream flavor, but you will pay a price at both the checkout and calorie counters. Most kinds available in grocery stores are ultra-pasteurized and contain emulsifiers and stabilizers.

Light cream. Also called coffee cream, light cream has 20 percent butterfat. It produces a relatively rich ice cream with fewer calories.

Half-and-half. A mixture of milk and cream with 12 percent butterfat, half-and-half makes a satisfactory ice cream with a hint of richness.

Whole milk. Fresh, whole milk contains 3½ percent butterfat. It is the basic ingredient in most ice creams and sherbets.

Low-fat milks. Low-fat (2 percent butterfat), 99 percent fat-free, and skim (less than ½ percent butterfat) milks are useful when you want to limit calories, but you will get a coarser texture in the ice cream.

Nonfat dry milk. An economical choice, nonfat dry milk is handy because it needs no refrigeration prior to reconstituting with water. Mix instant dry milk granules in the proportions recommended on the package. To reconstitute non-instant dry milk powder, combine 1 part powder with 4 parts water, or for a richer ice cream, use 2 parts powder. A blender works well for this, or first mix the powder with a small amount of water to form a paste before adding the remaining water.

Buttermilk. Originally the liquid leftover in the churn after butter was made, today buttermilk is made by adding a bacterial culture to pasteurized skim milk. Its thick, creamy texture, low calories, and tart flavor make it a useful ingredient in many frozen desserts.

Evaporated milk. Evaporated milk is made by removing some of the water from fresh milk, adding various chemical stabilizers; it is then sealed in cans and heat-sterilized. Used undiluted, evaporated milk gives a richer taste and smoother texture to ice cream than plain whole milk.

Yogurt. You can make yogurt with fresh whole, low-fat, skim, or nonfat dry milks and even soy milk. Frozen yogurt made with any of these products will have the characteristic tart, tangy flavor. It is very economical to make your own yogurt. If using purchased yogurt, be sure to buy brands with live bacterial cultures, preferably with no flavoring, or only those with preserves at the bottom and no additives.

Sour cream. Made from light cream and inoculated with a bacterial culture, commercially available sour creams may have texture-enhancing additives. Sour cream helps make ice cream rich and tangy.

Soy milk. As high in protein as cow's milk, soy milk has only one-third as much fat — and it is unsaturated fat to boot. When making ice cream, add ¼ cup vegetable oil for every 3 cups soy milk to make a richer product. Soy milk powder is available, or soy milk can be made by soaking soybeans overnight, grinding, cooking with water, and straining off the milk.

Sweeteners

Sweeteners enhance the taste and smell of food. Sugars are found in almost all plants and in two animal products, milk and honey. They are an important aspect of our diet in that they supply quick energy. Too much sugar, however, can have a harmful effect on one's health as well as adding unnecessary calories. Also, most of the products used to sweeten foods are highly refined and devoid of nutrients. It is better to rely on natural sugars found in fruits when making desserts, and to learn to appreciate foods that are less sweet.

Much controversy rages over the relative merits of various sweeteners. For simplicity, the recipes in this book call for the two most readily-used sweeteners, honey and white sugar. Other sweeteners can be easily substituted. A proportion of ¾ cup granulated white sugar or ⅓ cup honey to each 4 cups of dairy product is usual when making ice cream. Syrups and honey tend to give a smoother texture because they control crystal formation.

However, sugar also adds to the overall solids of the mixture in a way that is different from honey and syrups. A high solid content lowers the freezing point for the mixture, causing the ice cream to freeze more solid and be easier to scoop. Honey and syrups often have a higher moisture content than sugar which also affects the product. A little experimenting should give you an idea of the different results to be obtained by using various sweeteners.

Granulated white sugar. Granulated white sugar is the most common sweetener, however, it is totally devoid of nutrients.

Brown sugar. Brown sugar is white sugar with molasses added, which gives it traces of vitamins and minerals. Brown sugar adds a distinctive taste, and should be used in the same proportion as white sugar, though lightly packed.

Honey. Depending on its own taste, honey may add a slight or a strong flavor to your ice cream. Darker honeys are usually stronger and sweeter. Honey that is labeled unfiltered, raw, or uncooked will have traces of vitamins and minerals. Half as much honey is needed to sweeten ice cream as white sugar.

Sugar Substitutes

To make ice cream, 1 cup white sugar is equal to each of the following:
- ½ cup honey
- ½ cup molasses
- ⅔ cup maple syrup
- ⅓ cup crystalline fructose
- 1½ cups maltose
- ½ cup sorghum
- 1 cup brown sugar lightly packed

Unsulphured molasses. A by-product of the sugar refining process, molasses contains some iron, calcium, and phosphorus. It has a distinctive flavor that is appropriate only with certain flavors of ice cream. Use ½ cup of molasses for 1 cup of white sugar in recipes.

Maple syrup. This ingredient adds not only sugar, but also its own unique flavor to foods. Be sure to use only pure maple syrup, free of additives, not flavored pancake syrup. Substitute ⅔ cup maple syrup for 1 cup of white sugar.

Light corn syrup. Sometimes used in making fruit ices and sherbets, light corn syrup produces a light, smooth texture with no flavor effect. It is a mixture of refined sugars, partially digested starches, water, salt, and vanilla. A less expensive, homemade sugar syrup or honey may be preferred.

Dark corn syrup. A distinctive flavor, dark corn syrup has the same drawbacks as light corn syrup. Use dark honey or molasses instead.

Fructose. A sugar found naturally in fruit and honey, fructose does not have an adverse affect on a person's blood sugar level. As it is two-thirds sweeter than white sugar, it can be used in smaller quantities. Substitute ⅓ cup crystalline fructose for 1 cup sugar; liquid fructose varies in concentration, so follow label directions. Although called fruit sugar, the commercially available forms are usually made by extensive refining of corn, sugar beets, or sugar cane.

Maltose. Maltose is most frequently found as barley malt or rice syrup, both the cooked liquid of fermented grain and with a subtle flavor. It does not create blood sugar fluctuations, but maltose is less sweet than other sugars so more must be used. Substitute 1½ cups maltose for 1 cup of white sugar.

Sorghum. A molasses-like product, sorghum is made from a plant related to corn. When using sorghum substitute ½ cup sorghum for 1 cup of white sugar.

Flavorings

This is where your creativity really has a chance to flower in ice cream making. Always use pure extracts and the finest ingredients, whether it be vanilla, chocolate, carob, fruits, nuts, coffee, or liqueurs. Using home-grown fruits and nuts is not only a source of pride, but the way to be sure of the best ingredients at a reasonable cost.

Fillers, Stabilizers, and Emulsifiers

These make a smoother frozen product with smaller ice crystals. They also add body and richness, and increase the amount of air that can be incorporated. Since one of the reasons to make your own frozen desserts is to avoid additives, you may choose not to use these. But if you do, it's best to select ones that add to the nutritional content. Remember, though, these also add extra cost.

Eggs. An excellent inexpensive source of complete protein, eggs also contain certain minerals and vitamins. The egg yolks in custard ice cream help to thicken and add richness. Beaten egg whites also add body and richness as well as making a smoother, fluffier product. Ice creams with eggs also store longer in the freezer.

Cream of tartar. A natural fruit acid made from grapes, cream of tartar can be used to increase volume, to stabilize, and to firm egg whites. Add at the beginning of beating, using ¼ teaspoon to 2–4 whites.

Be Careful with Eggs

The U.S. Department of Agriculture strongly recommends that you **do not use** raw eggs, raw egg yolks or raw egg whites in making ice cream, in order to avoid salmonella poisoning. Use eggs only where they can be cooked. Cook all custard mixtures to a temperature of 160°F, to kill any possible bacteria.

Arrowroot. The powdered starch of several tropical plant roots, arrowroot is an excellent thickener, or filler. Easy to digest, it is clear when diluted and has no chalky taste like cornstarch. As arrowroot is more acid-stable than flour, it works well with fruit. It is effective at lower temperatures and when cooked for a shorter period of time than other thickeners. Use 1½ teaspoons arrowroot in place of 1 tablespoon flour or cornstarch.

Cornstarch. A finely milled corn with the germ removed, cornstarch may be used as a thickening agent in cooked custard mixtures to make a smoother ice cream. It has little food value. Use 1 tablespoon in 2 cups cooked liquid when making custard ice cream.

Whole wheat flour. Whole wheat flour can be used as a thickening agent in cooked custard mixtures to make a smoother ice cream. It will contribute a slight amount of food value. Use 1 tablespoon in 2 cups cooked liquid when making custard ice cream.

Unflavored gelatin. Unflavored gelatin is a protein extracted from animal parts, then dried and powdered. It helps to make a smoother ice cream. Dissolve it in water and cook before adding to other ingredients. Use 1½ teaspoons in a 1½ quart batch of ice cream.

Agar. A sea vegetable high in minerals, agar can be used in place of unflavored gelatin. Agar is available as a concentrated powder, flakes, or sticks, and unlike gelatin, it gels without requiring chilling. It is flavorless and highly absorptive. Use 1½ tablespoons to 1 quart of liquid.

Salt

Salt is frequently used in foods as it heightens and enhances flavors. While an essential element in the body's health, too much salt can cause problems. It can be omitted from ice cream with little notice.

Equipment

Ice cream freezers for home use come in sizes ranging from 1 quart to 2 gallons. Some are elaborate and expensive, but most are relatively inexpensive and still very functional. In deciding which ice cream freezer to buy, consider such factors as cost, when and how you want to use it, durability, portability, and storage space needed. A large freezer can be used to make small amounts as well as party-size quantities.

Old-fashioned ice cream churns. These churns are available as either hand-cranked models or as electricity powered units. A large plastic, fiberglass, or wood tub holds a smaller, metal can. The ice cream mixture is placed inside the can along with a dasher or paddle and the assembly is covered. To freeze the ice cream, a brine solution of ice and salt is placed in the tub around the metal can. Turning the crank-and-gear assembly on top of the can rotates the dasher or paddle and mixes the ice cream. The dasher extends the height of the can and scrapes the ice crystals at the edge of the can to the inside. Churning is usually finished in 20 minutes.

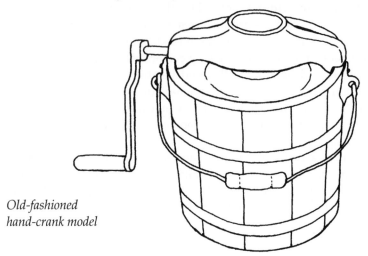

*Old-fashioned
hand-crank model*

In-freezer ice cream churn. Such churns include a 1-quart unit with a dasher, metal can, plastic tub, and electrical assembly that uses the frigid air of a deep freezer or refrigerator freezer rather than ice and salt to freeze the mixture inside. Churning is usually completed in 1½ hours.

Self-contained ice cream churns. These models come in sizes slightly more and slightly less than 1 quart. Using their own freon freezing unit and powdered electrically, they can make ice cream in 20 minutes. Although expensive, their ease of operation, speed, and lack of mess make them appealing.

With any of these machines, be sure to follow manufacturer's directions and care instructions. With all machines, it is important to wash, rinse, and thoroughly dry after each use. Wipe around electric motors and gear housings with a dampened, well-squeezed sponge followed by a dry towel.

Ice. Ice is cheapest when made at home. Plan ahead and make plenty, figuring on 8 ice cube trays or 6 pounds of ice to make 1½ quarts of ice cream. Ice can be crushed to provide the most surface area for heat exchange, but cubes work reasonably well. Ice can be crushed by putting in a burlap or other heavy sack and hitting with a hammer.

Salt. Salt lowers the freezing temperature of water. Use table salt with ice cubes, and coarser, more slowly dissolving rock salt with crushed ice. For a 1½-quart batch of ice cream, you will need 1½ cups table salt or 1 cup rock salt. Additional salt will be needed if the ice cream is hardened in the churn.

Other Equipment

Measuring spoons	Whisk
Measuring cups	Wooden spoon
Glass measuring cup	Electric mixer or rotary beater
Saucepan	Shallow pans such as 8-inch
Blender, food processor,	round or square cake pan
or food mill	or ice-cube tray
Fine strainer	Rubber bowl scraper
Glass, ceramic, or stainless	Freezer storage containers
steel bowls	

Basic Procedure for Churned Ice Cream

1. Prepare ice cream or other frozen dessert mixture, pour in bowl, cover, and chill for several hours in the refrigerator. This will give a smoother product with less freezing time.

2. Wash the dasher, lid, and can; rinse and dry. Place in the refrigerator to chill. Keeping the equipment cold will make the process of freezing your mixture go faster.

3. Pour chilled mixture into the can, making sure it is not more than two-thirds full to allow for expansion. Put on the lid.

4. Put the can into the freezer tub and attach the crank-and-gear assembly.

5. Fill the tub one-third full of ice. Sprinkle an even layer of salt on top about ⅛-inch thick. Continue adding ice and salt in the same proportions layer by layer until the tub is filled up to, but not over, the top of the can. The salt-to-ice ratio affects freezing temperature and, therefore, freezing time. Too much salt and the ice cream will freeze too quickly and be coarse; too little salt will keep the mixture from freezing. Many factors influence the ratio, but the best proportion seems to be 8 parts ice to 1 part salt, by weight.

6. If using ice cubes, add 1 cup of cold water to the ice-and-salt mixture to help the ice melt and settle. If using crushed ice, let the ice-packed tub set for 5 minutes before beginning to churn. While churning, add more ice and salt, in the same proportions as before, so that it remains up to the top of the can.

7. Start cranking slowly at first — slightly less than 1 revolution per second — until the mixture begins to pull. Then churn as quickly and as steadily as possible for 5 minutes. Finally, churn at a slightly slower rate for a few more minutes, or until the mixture turns reasonably hard.

8. For electrically powdered ice cream churns, fill can with mix and plug in the unit. Allow to churn until it stops in about 15 to 20 minutes. Most kinds have an automatic reset switch that will prevent motor damage by stopping when the ice

cream is ready. If the freezer becomes clogged with chunks of ice, the motor may shut off or stall. Restart by turning the can with your hands.

9. When the ice cream is ready, remove the crank-and-gear assembly. Wipe all ice and salt from the top. Remove the lid and lift out the beater. The ice cream should be the texture of mush. Scrape the cream from the beater. Add chopped nuts and fruit or sauce for ripple, if desired. Pack down the cream with a spoon. Cover with several layers of wax paper and replace the lid, putting a cork in the cover hole.

10. Ripen and harden the ice cream by placing in a deep-freezer or refrigerator freezer, or repack in the tub with layers of ice and salt until the can and lid are completely covered. Use more salt than for making the ice cream. Cover the freezer with a blanket or heavy towel and set in a cool place until ready to serve, about an hour.

Tips for Churn-Frozen Ice Cream

■ Make sure batter is well-chilled before freezing.
■ Never fill can more than three-quarters full; two-thirds is preferred.
■ If hand-cranking, be sure to start slowly until you feel a pull.
■ Proportions of salt to ice will vary according to content with those mixtures high in sugar or alcohol needing more salt and those low in sugar or high in butterfat needing less.

Basic Procedure for Still-Frozen Ice Cream

1. Prepare the ice cream mixture as directed and pour into a shallow tray such as a cake pan or ice-cube tray without the dividers.

2. Place the tray in the freezer compartment of the refrigerator at the coldest setting or a deep freezer for 30 minutes to 1 hour, or until the mixture is mushy but not solid.

3. Scrape the mixture into a chilled bowl and beat it with a rotary beater or electric mixer as rapidly as possible until the mixture is smooth.

4. Return the mixture to the tray and the freezer. When almost frozen solid, repeat the beating process. Add chopped nuts and fruits, liqueur, or ripple sauce, if desired.

5. Return to the tray and cover the cream with plastic wrap to prevent ice crystals from forming on top. Place in the freezer until solid.

Tips for Still-Frozen Ice Cream

- Use as little sweetener as possible.
- If using whipped cream, beat only to soft peaks for maximum volume and better flavor.
- If using whipped cream, add to mixture when well-chilled or partially frozen.
- Use lowest freezer temperature possible.
- Do not freeze ice cubes and ice cream at the same time in a refrigerator freezer.
- Have refrigerator freezer unit defrosted.
- Do not open the freezer door during freezing of the ice cream unless absolutely necessary.
- Add nuts and chunk fruits when the mixture is partially frozen.

Recipes

Each of these recipes makes 1½ quarts or about 6 servings. The recipes can be decreased or increased to accommodate smaller or larger ice cream freezers. If making still-frozen ice cream, these recipes will fill 2 shallow pans.

BASIC VANILLA ICE CREAM

Whether cooked or uncooked, this simple, fast version can be made as rich or as low-calorie as you desire. Variations are infinite.

- 1 quart heavy *or* light cream *or* half-and-half *or* 2 cups each heavy and light cream
- 1 cup sugar *or* ⅓ cup honey
- 1 tablespoon pure vanilla extract

The above ingredients can be mixed and used as is or the cream can be scalded. Scalding concentrates the milk solids and improves the flavor.

To scald, slowly heat cream in a saucepan until just below the boiling point. Small bubbles will begin to appear around the edges. Stir for several minutes, then remove from heat. Stir in the sweetener. Pour into a bowl, cover, and chill. When completely cooled, add the vanilla. When thoroughly chilled, follow directions for either churned or still-frozen ice cream.

VANILLA CUSTARD ICE CREAM

Although thickened and enriched with egg yolks, this recipe uses less cream and has a less striking vanilla taste. It, too, can be used as the basis for many different flavors.

- 2 cups milk
- 4 egg yolks
- ½ cup sugar *or* ¼ cup honey
- 1 tablespoon pure vanilla extract
- 2 cups heavy cream

Heat milk to scalding. In the top part of a double boiler, whisk together egg yolks and sugar until thick and smooth. Slowly pour the hot milk into the egg mixture, beating constantly. Place the pan over the lower part of the double boiler filled with gently simmering water. Stirring constantly, cook until slightly thickened. Remove from heat and cool. Strain into a bowl and add the vanilla extract and cream. Chill thoroughly. Follow directions for either churned or still-frozen ice cream.

Variations on the Basic Recipe

- **Super-Smooth Vanilla Ice Cream**

  To the Vanilla Custard Ice Cream recipe: whip the cream to soft peaks before folding into the cooled custard mixture.

- **Super Creamy Vanilla Ice Cream**

  To the Basic Vanilla Ice Cream recipe: soften 1½ teaspoons unflavored gelatin in ¼ cup water and add with sugar to scalded milk. Continue cooking over low heat until gelatin is dissolved. Or, substitute 1½ tablespoons agar.

- **Ice Milk**

  To the Basic Vanilla or Vanilla Custard Ice Cream recipe, substitute whole, low-fat, skim, or reconstituted dry milk for the cream.

- **Ice Buttermilk**

  To the Basic Vanilla Ice Cream recipe, substitute buttermilk for the cream and do not scald.

- **Ice Sour Cream**

  To the Basic Vanilla Ice Cream recipe, substitute sour cream for the cream and do not scald.

- **Ice Soy Milk**

  To the Basic Vanilla Ice Cream recipe, substitute soy milk for the cream, without scalding. Combine soy milk, sweetener, flavoring, and ¼ cup vegetable oil and whirl in a blender.

Beyond Vanilla

Once you're mastered vanilla, you will want to try these quick and easy flavor variations.

APPLESAUCE-RAISIN-SPICE-NUT ICE CREAM

To the Basic Vanilla or Vanilla Custard Ice Cream recipe: add 1½ cups applesauce and ¼ teaspoon each ground nutmeg, cinnamon, and cloves. Soak ½ cup raisins in water or brandy to cover until plump. Drain, chop, and add with ¾ cup chopped pecans or walnuts to ice cream when it has become mushy. This recipe is especially good made with sour cream.

AVOCADO ICE CREAM

To the Basic Vanilla Ice Cream recipe: omit vanilla and add 1 tablespoon lemon juice and 1½ cups pureed avocado to the cream mixture just before freezing.

BANANA ICE CREAM

To the Basic Vanilla or Vanilla Custard Ice Cream recipe: add 1 tablespoon lemon juice and 1½ cups mashed banana to the cream mixture just before freezing.

BANANA-NUT ICE CREAM

To Banana Ice Cream recipe: add ¾ cup chopped nuts to ice cream when it has become mushy.

BRANDIED CHERRY ICE CREAM

To the Basic Vanilla Ice Cream recipe: add 1½ cups pureed fresh dark sweet cherries to the cream mixture just before freezing. Omit the vanilla and add ½ teaspoon almond extract and ½ cup kirschwasser, or cherry, or chocolate cherry liqueur.

BRANDY ALEXANDER ICE CREAM

To the Basic Vanilla Ice Cream recipe: omit the vanilla and add ¼ cup each brandy and crème de cacao to the cream mixture just before freezing.

BURNT ALMOND ICE CREAM

To the Basic Vanilla or Vanilla Custard ice Cream recipe: substitute light brown sugar, lightly packed, for white sugar. Toast 1 cup blanched, chopped almonds in a 350°F oven until golden and add when ice cream is mushy.

BUTTER PECAN ICE CREAM

To the Basic Vanilla or Vanilla Custard Ice Cream recipe: add to the mushy ice cream ⅔ cup chopped pecans that have been sautéed in 3 tablespoons butter until golden.

BUTTERSCOTCH ICE CREAM

To the Basic Vanilla or Vanilla Custard Ice Cream recipe: substitute lightly packed brown sugar for white sugar, cooking it with 2 tablespoons butter until butter melts. Boil 1 minute and carefully stir into heated milk. Stirring, cook until well blended.

BUTTERSCOTCH-PECAN ICE CREAM

To Butterscotch Ice Cream: add ¾ cup chopped pecans when the ice cream is mushy.

CARAMEL ICE CREAM

To the Basic Vanilla or Vanilla Custard Ice Cream recipe: melt the sugar called for in the recipes in a heavy skillet until golden. Carefully pour in ½ cup boiling water. Stir until dissolved and boil for 10 minutes, or until thick. Add to hot cream mixture.

CAROB ICE CREAM

To the Basic Vanilla or Vanilla Custard Ice Cream recipe: melt 8 ounces of carob nuggets in a small pan over low heat and add to scalded milk.

CAROB CHIP ICE CREAM

To the Basic Vanilla or Vanilla Custard Ice Cream recipe: add 1 cup finely chopped carob nuggets to cream mixture just before freezing.

CAROB-COCONUT ICE CREAM

To Carob Ice Cream: add ¼ cup shredded coconut when ice cream is mushy.

CAROB-COFFEE ICE CREAM

To Carob Ice Cream: mix 2 tablespoons instant coffee, espresso, or grain beverage with 3 tablespoons hot water, or use ½ cup brewed coffee and add to warm cream mixture before chilling.

CAROB-RAISIN-NUT ICE CREAM

To Carob Ice Cream: add ½ cup raisins that have been soaked in water, brandy, or rum, drained, and chopped, and ½ cup chopped nuts when ice cream is mushy.

CHESTNUT ICE CREAM

To the Basic Vanilla or Vanilla Custard Ice Cream recipe: add 1 cup unsweetened chestnut puree to warm cream mixture before chilling.

CHOCOLATE ICE CREAM

To the Basic Vanilla or Vanilla Custard Ice Cream recipe: melt two to six 1-ounce squares of bitter or semi-sweet chocolate (depending on personal preference) in a small pan over low heat and add to scalded milk. Increase sugar to taste, usually doubling the standard quantity.

CHOCOLATE CHIP ICE CREAM

To the Basic Vanilla or Vanilla Custard Ice Cream recipe: add 1 cup finely chopped chocolate chips to cream mixture just before freezing.

CHOCOLATE-COCONUT ICE CREAM

To Chocolate Ice Cream: add ⅓ cup shredded coconut when ice cream is mushy.

CHOCOLATE-RAISIN-NUT ICE CREAM

To Chocolate Ice Cream: add ½ cup raisins that have been soaked until plump in water, brandy, or rum, drained, and chopped, and ½ cup chopped nuts when ice cream is mushy.

CITRUS ICE CREAM

To the Basic Vanilla or Vanilla Custard ice Cream recipe: omit vanilla and 1 cup milk or cream and add the juice of a lemon, lime, and orange and 1 teaspoon grated rind of each fruit to the cream mixture just before freezing.

COFFEE ICE CREAM

To the Basic Vanilla or Vanilla Custard Ice Cream recipe: add 3 tablespoons instant coffee, espresso, or grain beverage dissolved in 4 tablespoons hot water, or ¾ cup brewed coffee to cream mixture just before freezing.

COFFEE-WALNUT ICE CREAM

To Coffee Ice Cream, add ¾ cup chopped walnuts when the ice cream is mushy.

EGGNOG ICE CREAM

To Vanilla Custard Ice Cream: add 3 tablespoons rum, brandy, or bourbon just before freezing.

FRUIT ICE CREAM

To the Basic Vanilla or Vanilla Custard Ice Cream recipe: add just before freezing 1½ cups fruit puree stirred with 2 teaspoons fresh lemon juice to heighten flavor and 2 tablespoons sugar or 1 tablespoon honey.

Use fresh or unsweetened frozen fruit such as strawberries, peaches, apricots, cherries, blueberries, raspberries, blackberries, mangoes, or plums. If you use pineapple, be sure to use canned, not fresh, pineapple. Fresh pineapple contains an acid that breaks down proteins, including milk protein, and will keep your ice cream from hardening properly. Fruits with seeds such as raspberries or blackberries should be drained after pureeing.

GINGER ICE CREAM

To Basic Vanilla or Vanilla Custard Ice Cream recipe: add ½ cup finely chopped preserved ginger and 3 tablespoons ginger syrup when adding vanilla to chilled cream mixture.

GRASSHOPPER ICE CREAM

To the Basic Vanilla Ice Cream recipe: add ¼ cup each green crème de menthe and crème de cacao to chilled cream mixture just before freezing.

MAPLE-WALNUT ICE CREAM

To the Basic Vanilla or Vanilla Custard Ice Cream recipe: use ½ cup pure maple syrup for the sweetener and add ¾ cup chopped walnuts when ice cream is mushy.

MINT ICE CREAM

To the Basic Vanilla or Vanilla Custard Ice Cream recipe: reduce vanilla extract to 1 teaspoon and add 2 teaspoons peppermint extract to chilled cream mixture. Add several drops of green food coloring, if desired.

MINT CHOCOLATE OR CAROB CHIP

To the Mint Ice Cream recipe: add 1 cup finely chopped chocolate or carob chips to cream mixture just before freezing.

MOCHA ICE CREAM

To the Chocolate Ice Cream recipe: mix 2 tablespoons instant coffee, espresso, or grain beverage with 3 tablespoons hot water, or use ½ cup brewed coffee and add to warm cream mixture before chilling.

MOCHA-SPICE ICE CREAM

To the Mocha Ice Cream recipe: add ½ teaspoon each ground cinnamon and ground cloves to warm cream mixture before chilling.

NUT BRITTLE ICE CREAM

To the Basic Vanilla or Vanilla Custard Ice Cream recipe: add, when the ice cream is mushy, ½ pound crushed and pulverized nut brittle.

ORANGE ICE CREAM

To the Basic Vanilla or Vanilla Custard Ice Cream recipe: reduce milk or cream by 1 cup and add 1 cup orange juice and 1 teaspoon grated orange rind.

ORANGE CHOCOLATE OR CAROB CHIP ICE CREAM

To the Orange Ice Cream recipe: add 1 cup finely chopped chocolate or carob chips to cream mixture just before freezing.

ORANGE LIQUEUR ICE CREAM

To the Orange Ice Cream recipe: add ½ cup orange liqueur such as Triple-Sec or Grand Marnier just before freezing.

ORANGE-SPICE-CHOCOLATE ICE CREAM

To the Chocolate Ice Cream recipe: add 1 tablespoon grated orange rind, ¼ teaspoon almond extract, and ½ teaspoon ground cinnamon just before freezing.

PEACH-PECAN ICE CREAM

To the Fruit Ice Cream recipe using peaches: add ¾ cup chopped pecans when the ice cream is mushy.

PEANUT BUTTER ICE CREAM

To the Basic Vanilla or Vanilla Custard Ice Cream recipe: heat 1 cup plain or chunky-style peanut butter with the milk, blending thoroughly.

PEANUT BUTTER CHOCOLATE OR CAROB CHIP ICE CREAM

To the Peanut Butter Ice Cream recipe, add 1 cup finely chopped chocolate or carob chips to cream mixture just before freezing.

PECAN PRALINE ICE CREAM

To the Basic Vanilla or Vanilla Custard Ice Cream recipe: lightly coat an 8-inch cake pan with vegetable oil and put in 1 cup chopped pecans. In a heavy skillet, slowly melt ½ cup sugar with 1 tablespoon water, stirring occasionally, until the mixture turns a light brown. Pour over the pecans. When the caramel has hardened, break it into very small pieces. Add to the ice cream when mushy.

PEPPERMINT CANDY ICE CREAM

To the Basic Vanilla or Vanilla Custard Ice Cream recipe: add ¼ cup crushed peppermint stick candy to the milk while it heats, stir until dissolved. Add 1 teaspoon peppermint extract to chilled cream mixture. Stir in ¼ cup crushed peppermint stick candy to ice cream mixture when mushy.

PERSIMMON ICE CREAM

To the Basic Vanilla Custard Ice Cream recipe: add 1 cup seeded, pureed wild persimmons and 2 tablespoons lemon juice to the warm custard mixture.

PISTACHIO ICE CREAM

To the Basic Vanilla or Vanilla Custard Ice Cream recipe: add 1 teaspoon almond extract with the vanilla extract. Add 1 cup finely chopped pistachio nuts when the ice cream is mushy. If you want green ice cream, add several drops of green food coloring with the extracts.

PUMPKIN ICE CREAM

To the Basic Vanilla Custard Ice Cream recipe: substitute lightly packed brown sugar or molasses for sugar and beat into the warm custard mixture 2 cups pumpkin puree, 1 teaspoon ground cinnamon, and ¼ teaspoon each ground ginger, ground cloves, and ground nutmeg.

RHUBARB ICE CREAM

To the Basic Vanilla or Vanilla Custard Ice Cream recipe: cook 2 pounds diced fresh rhubarb with 1 cup sugar or ½ cup honey and 1 tablespoon grated lemon rind until soft, then puree and chill. Add to the cream mixture just before freezing.

ROCKY ROAD ICE CREAM

To any Chocolate or Carob ice cream: add ½ cup chopped nuts and ½ cup marshmallow bits to ice cream when mushy.

RUM-RAISIN ICE CREAM

To the Basic Vanilla or Vanilla Custard Ice Cream recipe: soak ⅔ cup raisins in rum to cover until plump. Drain and dice raisins. Add rum and diced raisins to ice cream when mushy.

SWIRL ICE CREAM

To the Basic Vanilla or Vanilla Custard Ice Cream recipe or another appropriate recipe: remove dasher after freezer stops. With a knife or narrow spatula, stir in 1 cup thick dessert sauce or jam just enough to create a swirl effect. Use dessert sauces such as caramel, butterscotch, blueberry, carob, chocolate, or marshmallow, and jams such as strawberry, blackberry, raspberry, peach, apricot, or apple butter.

TOASTED COCONUT ICE CREAM

To the Basic Vanilla or Vanilla Custard Ice Cream recipe: add 1 cup lightly toasted shredded coconut to the cream mixture when mushy.

TROPICAL FRUIT ICE CREAM

To the Basic Vanilla or Vanilla Custard Ice Cream recipe: add ¾ cup orange juice, ¼ cup lemon juice, ½ cup mashed banana, and ½ cup canned, crushed pineapple to the cream mixture just before freezing. Do not use fresh pineapple, or your ice cream will not harden properly.

Sherbets

The differences between sherbets, sorbets, and ices is ambiguous and open to much culinary debate. They are as variable as the cook and the country of origin.

Basically, these desserts consist of fruit puree or juice, sweetener, and water or milk. They may be churned or still-frozen. Gelatin can be used to make a product that is smooth in body, but these are supposed to be somewhat coarse in texture so it really isn't necessary. Using a sugar syrup, honey, or other syrup form of sweetener is recommended for the positive effect on texture.

However sherbets and their cousins are distinguished and made, the result is an intensely flavored, refreshing treat. They are particularly delightful as a light dessert, during summer's hot days, or any time you're counting calories. The citrus and wine ices are also often used between courses of a dinner to cleanse the palate.

MILK SHERBET

½   cup simple syrup *or* ¼ cup honey
2   cups fruit puree or juice
2   tablespoons lemon juice
2   cups milk (whole, 2 percent, low-fat, skim, buttermilk, or reconstituted dry)

To make simply syrup, combine ⅓ cup sugar and ⅓ cup water in a small saucepan and cook over medium heat until sugar is dissolved. Remove from heat just before syrup comes to a boil. When the mixture is cool, cover and chill in refrigerator.

Combine sugar syrup, honey, or other sweetener with the pureed fruit or juice, lemon juice, and milk. The mixture may appear curdled, but it won't affect the final product. Chill thoroughly, then follow the basic procedure for either churned or still-frozen ice cream.

Sherbet Variations

ICE SHERBET

1   cup simple syrup *or* ½ cup honey
3   cups fruit puree or juice
2   tablespoons lemon juice

Prepare simple syrup as above, using ⅔ cup sugar and ⅔ cup water, or use honey or other sweetener. Combine sweetener, fruit puree or juice, and lemon juice. Chill thoroughly, then follow the basic procedure for either the churned or still-frozen ice cream.

SMOOTHER SHERBET

Stir 1 envelope unflavored gelatin or 1 tablespoon agar into ¼ cup cold water, add to syrup or sweetener, and cook for a few minutes until dissolved. Proceed as above. When sherbet has been churned for about 15 minutes (or when ready for first beating if still-frozen), fold in 2 stiffly beaten egg whites.

CREAMY SHERBET

To the basic Milk Sherbet recipe: substitute half-and-half, light, or heavy cream for the milk.

SOY SHERBET

To the basic Milk Sherbet recipe: substitute soy milk plus 2 tablespoons vegetable oil for the milk, blending thoroughly.

FRUIT SHERBET

To the basic Milk or Ice Sherbet recipes: use puree or juice of such fruits as lemon, lime, orange, grapefruit, grape, apricot, plum, apple, pear, grape, peach, strawberry, blackberry, raspberry, or melon. If using milk or gelatin, use only canned pineapple; fresh pineapple will prevent the sherbet from gelling properly. Fresh pineapple should not have any adverse effects on sherbet made only with water.

Strain out seeds of such fruits as blackberry or raspberry. To make Rhubarb or Cranberry Sherbet, cook the fruit first in a small quantity of water before pureeing.

COFFEE SHERBET

To the basic Milk or Ice Sherbet recipe: substitute coffee for the juice.

WINE SHERBET

To the basic Milk or Ice Sherbet recipe: substitute for part of the milk, cream or water any wine such as white, red, rose, fortified, fruit, or berry. Prior to adding to the mixture, bring it first to a boil for 3 minutes in a wide, shallow pan to drive off the alcohol so it will freeze.

FROZEN YOGURT

Yogurt's unique taste has made it a favorite frozen dessert. Commercial brands are expensive and often loaded with additives and calories. Making your own frozen yogurt, especially with your own homemade yogurt, is a delicious, yet economical, treat.

BASIC VANILLA FROZEN YOGURT

4   cups plain yogurt (made with whole, 2 percent, low-fat, skim, reconstituted dry, or soy milk)

¼–½ cup honey *or* other sweetener, to taste

1   tablespoon pure vanilla extract

Combine ingredients in a blender or with a mixer to make a light, smooth mixture. Follow procedure for churned or still-frozen ice cream.

Frozen Yogurt Variations

SMOOTHER FROZEN YOGURT

To the Basic Vanilla Frozen Yogurt recipe: soften 1½ teaspoons unflavored gelatin or 1½ tablespoons agar in ¼ cup cold water. Cook over low heat until dissolved completely. Add to above ingredients.

FRUIT-FLAVORED FROZEN YOGURT

To the Basic Vanilla Frozen Yogurt recipe: omit the vanilla and add 2 cups pureed unsweetened fresh, frozen, or canned fruit or juice.

FLAVORED FROZEN YOGURT

To the Basic Vanilla Frozen Yogurt recipe: follow any of the Ice Cream or Sherbet recipes, substituting yogurt of the milk, cream, or other dairy product.

Other Storey Titles You Will Enjoy

101 Perfect Chocolate Chip Cookies, by Gwen Steege.
The best melt-in-your-mouth variations of the classic
favorite, selected from thousands of entries.

500 Treasured Country Recipes,
by Martha Storey & Friends.
Hundreds of recipes to stock your pantry and put together
great meals, each one with country soul.

Apple Cookbook, by Olwen Woodier.
More than 140 recipes to put everyone's favorite
fruit into tasty new combinations.

Candy Construction, by Sharon Bowers.
Delightful fantasy creations made from store-bought
candy and cookies.

Homemade Soda, by Andrew Schloss.
Recipes for a spectacular variety of fizzy juices, sparkling waters,
root beers, colas, and other carbonated concoctions.

Maple Syrup Cookbook, by Ken Haedrich.
Recipes both sweet and savory that feature maple
syrup and its wonderful earthy, tangy qualities.

Join the conversation. Share your experience with this book, learn more about
Storey Publishing's authors, and read original essays and book excerpts at storey.com.
Look for our books wherever quality books are sold or by calling 800-441-5700.